BOI
UNFORGIVENESS

Gillian Henriques

CONTENT   PAGE

Acknowedgement

There are people without whom this book would not be possible, and I want to extend my sincerest gratitude to them.

Thanks to my husband and children who are always there to support and help me in all I do.

Thanks to the Reverend Doctor Kenroy Wedderburn, my brother and Pastor, who have dedicated his time to proof read this book to ensure it is in line with the Word of God.

Thanks to Teresa Citro for her help in the summary of this book and her encouragement and support.

Thanks to the Father, Son and Holy Spirit, the triune God, whom I love and have committed my life to obey, and who have given me the ability, strength, knowledge and experience that I needed to make this book a reality.

Introduction

Digesting what God had to say about unforgiveness was not easy. However, I quickly realized that arguing with, or questioning God was not going to change His principles. Instead, I decided to do an intense study into God's Word and ask Him for guidance and strength to accept and undertand what He was trying to teach me.

It was sometime in 2010 that I wrote my first article on unforgiveness. Somehow I knew God had a message for me first, and then to all I can reach with this message. I shared the article I wrote, "The Dangers of Unforgivenes," on my ministry Facebook page with a hope to begin spreading this message. God was not nearly finished teaching me yet.

Step by step, over the many months that followed, God began showing me how truly dangerous it is to harbour this sin. Not only can unforgiveness rob you of your place in heaven, but it can also rob you of true liberty here on earth. Unforgiveness can prevent you from walking in the abundant life that Christ has for you.

Unforgiveness' danger became evident to me when God showed me that this is a sin with which all men will battle. As long as you are born on this earth, at some point you will be faced with the choice of forgiving an offender or not forgiving an offender.

Every man will be offended or hurt by another. The burden of choice is what decides your very fate. Will you forgive and be free, or will you harbor unforgiveness and be bound?

It is my hope that all who read it will choose to forgive rather than not. In the pages of this book, you will learn what unforgiveness is, how to identify it, how God views it, and how to overcome it.

Christ, who is love, and who died to set us free, expects nothing less than a forgiving heart of His children.

CHAPTER 1

What is Unforgiveness

"For if you forgive men their trespasses, your heavenly Father will also forgive you. But if you do not forgive men their trespasses, neither will your Father forgive your trespasses" (Matthew 6:14-15).

Unforgiveness is the most difficult word to define, though used so often. This is simply because people do not understand the magnitude of unforgiveness and the destruction it can cause, both to the one who has not forgiven and to the unforgiven. We glibly say things like, "I have forgiven him, but I will never forget what he has done," or, "I have forgiven him, but I do not want him in my life. I will never speak to him again, not after what he did to me." Certainly, these statements and ones similar to them prove that we do not know what unforgiveness is. Unforgiveness goes way deeper, and is far more destructive than we think.

Jesus, after teaching the simplest yet most profound prayer, "Our Father," says to His disciples, *"For if you forgive men their trespasses, your heavenly Father will also forgive you, but if you do not forgive men their trespasses, neither will your Father forgive your trespasses."*

A simple prayer it seems, but one that encompasses so many things. *"Forgive us our trespasses as we forgive those that trespass against us."* What is Jesus saying? God forgives you as you forgive. If you do not forgive, you will not get forgiveness of God. Thus, your prayer ought to be, "forgive us as we forgive."

Unforgiveness simply put, is holding a grudge against someone who has offended you. However its meaning is far more than this. People who have not forgiven will emphatically tell you, 'I am not holding a grudge. I have forgiven." Most people think that unforgiveness will cause you to think and act evil, or do evil against the person that you have not forgiven. Though this is true, it is not necessarily so all the time. You can have unforgiveness in your heart and still appear to be kind to the person you have not forgiven.

I once had a friend who did me wrong. I kept thinking, *after all I have done for her, how could she do this to me?* I knew God wanted me to, so I decided to forgive her. She would still talk to me, and I would talk to her too, but only saying a line or two each time. I was not willing to hold long conversations with her, or even allow her close to my heart again. Perhaps she was thinking that she was still my friend because I was still talking to her.

I was kind and courteous and friendly. However, in my heart I was saying,

"You'll never get the chance to do to me what you did before."

God spoke to me,

"You have not forgiven her."

"Of course I have forgiven her, I still speak to her." I said.

"Yes but your heart is not totally set free. Every time you have a conversation with your friend, or you happen to see her, or hear her name, your mind begins to rehearse what she did to you. You are still hurt, you push her away, and you have not forgiven." God replied.

"God you are right, I know I actually have to talk about this and forgive my friend," I thought.

How many times do you say you have forgiven someone, a friend, or a loved one, yet you constantly rehearse what they have done in your head? It is at the forefront of your mind, or perhaps somewhere buried way in the back - hidden. Either way you push that person away and decide they will never get close to your heart again.

There are other persons who have blatant unforgiveness. You have decided in your heart that the hurt is too great for you to forgive.

"So Esau hated Jacob because of the blessing with which his father blessed him, and Esau said in his heart, "The days of mourning for my father are at hand; then I will kill my brother Jacob" (Genesis 27:41).

Sometimes unforgiveness causes hatred to burn in our hearts so much that we want the person gone. We may not desire to kill them, but we secretly wish they were dead. Esau gave over his birthright to his brother for a plate of food. Then when his brother got the blessing, he hated him. Yes, of course Jacob tricked Esau, and then their father Isaac into giving the blessing he intended for Esau to him. To Esau, Jacob committed the unpardonable sin. *How could my own brother do that to me?* He was prepared to kill as unforgiveness caused rage to arise in his heart.

Unforgiveness is so dangerous it can make you into a literal murderer. When you begin to harbor thoughts like this, it has become more than just a grudge. You are treading on serious grounds. You must go before the Father and ask Him to remove this rage of unforgiveness from you.

Sometimes you think you do not hate the Unforgiven, you just want to escape them. You say,

"I have forgiven them, but the further away they are from me the better it is for me."

You totally remove yourself from that person. You do not speak to them, but your conscience sets you free by telling you that you are being wise, and are doing what is best for you. Only it is not about you, it is about doing the will of your Father. The will of the Father is straightforward... Forgive!

"Follow peace with all men, and holiness, without which no man shall see the Lord," (Hebrews 12:14).

Follow, search after or fight for peace. This is what God instructs. It goes further to say that if you do not have peace with everyone, including those who hurt you, you will not see God.

When I was a little girl our church had a crusade. My favorite preacher was on that night; every time he preached I got excited. *He is so on fire*, I thought. He was one of those preachers who shouted and jumped about and got excited and got you excited too. Of course, I was anxious to hear him. I made sure I was in the front row. I will never forget what he said that night,

"If you are going to sin, be a sinner, and make sure you do it well as persisting in one sin will separate you from God."

In other words, it makes no sense saying you are living for God and allow your unwillingness to let go of one sin to cause eternal separation.

Unforgiveness is a subtle sin. It is a trap of the enemy and a sin that will hold you bound. Let go and forgive.

Unforgiveness can be totally hidden. This is one of the reasons it becomes dangerous. You can think that you have forgiven someone; the person is still a part of your life; you still love that person, and you are sure you have forgiven them. Many years have passed, and you have the slightest disagreement, then you find that the thing that you thought you had forgiven resurface. The old wounds open up. The disagreement has nothing to do with that long time hurt, but suddenly it is a part of the argument. Because the hurt ran so deep, things escalate beyond what it should be. This often happens with close relatives, spouses, siblings, parents or children. Afterwards you sit and wonder from where did that come? That was not even what the disagreement was about. At other times, you justify yourself. He deserves it; He had it coming to him for what he did to me.

Unforgiveness is not letting go of the hurt and the pain. It is burying the pain so far away in your heart without dealing with it. It is always having the memory at the forefront of your mind, and totally loathing the Unforgiven. It is not hating, but barring your heart and pushing away the unforgiven. Unforgiveness comes in many forms and many ways. We have to learn to identify it.

"Looking diligently lest any man fail of the grace of God; lest any root of bitterness springing up trouble you, and thereby many be defiled" (Hebrews 12:15).

This Scripture comes directly after the one that says, seek peace with all men. Sometimes you may think you have made peace, but be diligent is the warning. Ensure bitterness has not taken root in you. If it has it will defile many.

Did you notice that the Scripture did not say it will defile you only? It says it will defile many. Often we do not keep secret unforgiveness. It is in the nature of man to talk about things, for want of putting it mildly. When you talk to someone else about what a person has done to you, even without meaning any harm, then it might cause that person to be bitter against the one of whom you speak.

Unforgiveness puts you into a trap and it holds you bound. You are not totally set free. It is a sin and so we must be prepared to forsake it as we forsake all other sins. As long as you hold on to unforgiveness, you are living in sin. What is even more frightening is that Jesus says in Matthew 6:14-15, you will not be forgiven by God. You know how we humans are, how we sin often. Imagine every time you sin and ask forgiveness, you think you are forgiven as you get off your knees, but God is waiting for you to forgive the one who have wronged you; therefore, you still have that sin.

CHAPTER 2

How You Got to a State of Unforgiveness

"Wherefore, my beloved brethren, let every man be swift to hear, slow to speak, slow to wrath: For the wrath of man worketh not the righteousness of God" (James 1:19-20).

As human beings, there is no escaping offense. I always say, in comfort of myself, that every man has a fault including me. Recognizing that I too am faulty makes it easier to bear the faults of my brother. We are all born in sin and shaped in iniquity and are therefore riddled with faults.

Adam fell and plunged the whole race into sin. Because of this fact, at some point or another we are bound to offend someone, and to be offended by someone. It is this constant reiterating of offense that brings about anger and hurt. Anger and hurt not dealt with leads to unforgiveness.

James says, *be quick to hear but slow to speak.* James seemed to have been often stung by the tongue, so much that he wrote about it emphatically throughout the book of James in the Bible. Many people have not mastered the art of remaining silent, so our tongue often gets us in trouble. The person who is first to start throwing insults is often the one who is first to be offended.

"But the tongue can no man tame, it is an unruly evil full of deadly poison" (James 3:8).

After exhorting us to be slow to speak in chapter 1, James was quick to point out that you cannot tame the tongue. Try saying nothing, James advises. You cannot manage to control what you say, so keep silent. Bite your tongue, we often say, or count to ten, but whatever you do try not to speak. It is often when we speak that we hurt someone, or even end up being hurt. When the tongue begins spewing its deadly venom someone is going to be offended.

"Let no corrupt communication proceed out of your mouth, but that which is good to the use of edifying, that it may minister grace unto the hearers" (Ephesians 4:29).

Again we are being warned about what comes out of our mouth. Many times we could have prevented an argument if we spoke with grace. We could have avoided hurting.

Hurt is the soil in which unforgiveness is planted.

There are times when no words are spoken and yet we are offended and we are hurt. I'm not so sure about men, but I know women are masters of using their actions to punish and teach lessons. I am usually terribly afraid when I go among a group of women, as unpleasant as it sounds. By their silence, they inflict wounds far deeper than any word could achieve. Hence the saying, "actions speak louder than words."

A person will give you the cold shoulder, undermine you, lambast you, ignore you, and break you down without saying a word. This can be one of the most painful hurts. When someone has done something to you that you think is unjust. When you believe that you are being treated unfairly. When you are lied on, talked about, belittled, among other things, you become angry and hurt. You can begin to resent the person who did you wrong.

"The wrath or anger of man does not produce the righteousness of God."

When you become angry, if that anger is harbored and allowed to become hurt, and you don't act swiftly surely you will find yourself with a cloak of unrighteousness. The seed of unforgiveness can be sown before you know it.

"Beloved, think it not strange concerning the fiery trial which is to try you, as though some strange thing happened unto you: But rejoice, inasmuch as ye are partakers of Christ's sufferings; that, when his glory shall be revealed, ye may be glad also with exceeding joy" (1 Peter 4:12-13).

It is testings that makes you strong. Therefore, everyone will be tested. One of the greatest tests you'll ever face is how you react or respond after someone has said or done something against you. Are they right to do you wrong? They are by no means right, but Peter says think it not strange when the test comes. We suffer because Christ suffers, and we must share in His suffering in order to share in His glory. Many people said things about Jesus. The Pharisees criticized Him every day. Even His closest friends betrayed Him.

Judas and Peter walked with Jesus. They were among the twelve closest persons to Jesus. Still, one betrayed Him, and the other denied Him. When He needed them most, they were not there. Judas collected thirty pieces of silver to point Him out with a kiss, and Peter swore he did not know Him.

The people that you least expect to hurt you will hurt you.

She was my closest friend yet look what she did to me. He said he loved me, but he lied to me. He was my best buddy, and he stabbed me in the back. She is family; she is the last person I expect to do that.

Your own mother, father, and siblings will hurt you? It does not matter from where the hurt come, the crucial thing is, in what state do you find yourself after you are hurt? Are you going to forgive, or remain in unforgiveness? You must be willing to deal with your hurt feelings in a way that you do not harbor any form of unforgiveness in your heart.

CHAPTER 3

How to Deal With Hurt and Persecution

"But I say unto you, Love your enemies, bless them that curse you, do good to them that hate you, and pray for them which despitefully use you, and persecute you" (Matthew 5:44).

Anger often leads to hurt. Someone may say something to, or about you, and you get angry, then you become offended, the offense takes root and becomes hurt.

Unfortunately, once hurt many people have no idea what to do. What we are prone to do is to leave angry after an argument or dispute, or after hearing something someone said or did. Then our mind comes into play. It begins telling us how awful that person is, how cruel, how rude.

"Be ye angry, and sin not: let not the sun go down upon your wrath: Neither give place to the devil" (Ephesians 4:26-27).

How do you get angry and do not sin? You have to deal with it. The Scripture above tells us exactly how. Do not let the sun go down and you are still angry. The devil will take that anger and use it against you, and sow hurt in your heart. Before you know it, you are filled with unforgiveness.

The Battle is in Your Mind, Bring Every Thought Captive

"Casting down imaginations, and every high thing that exalteth itself against the knowledge of God, and bringing into captivity every thought to the obedience of Christ; and having in a readiness to revenge all disobedience, when your obedience is fulfilled" (2 Corinthians 10:5-6).

It is not going to be easy to be angry and not allow it to fester into hurt feelings. It is even harder once you are hurt to overcome that hurt. The feeling of hurt is not the sin. What is sinful is when it is harbored, and becomes unforgiveness. The process that we often experience is anger, hurt, and then unforgiveness. The Scripture is careful to say, be very slow to get angry because it is not easy to be angry and not sin. The battle is often in our minds.

Let's say, for example, someone comes to you and tell you that a real good friend of yours said something hurtful about you behind your back. It may be, or may not be true. You start thinking, *how could he do that, he's is supposed to be my friend?* In your mind a battle begins to rage. Then you begin to get angry. That anger almost immediately converts to hurt. It does not stop there. Your mind is racing. Depending on who you are, you may or may not confront your friend. Either way your thoughts are constantly on what you just heard. The more you think about it the more anger and hurt develops. The more you think about the things you did for that person, the things you went through together, how you always have his back, how you would never think of betraying, or talking bad about him, is the more you get entangled in the web of unforgiveness.

You may begin to look at all his faults, *who does he think he is?* You begin to compare yourself with him. H*e is saying that about me...what about the time when he...* and there continue a raging battle that if not stopped, breeds dangerous unforgiveness.

The Bible exhorts us to take every thought captive and force it to obey Christ. In this instance we know what the Bible says, we must forgive. So we must actively force those thoughts about our offender out of our minds and begin quoting what God says in His word:

"And be ye kind one to another, tenderhearted, forgiving one another, even as God for Christ's sake hath forgiven you," (Ephesians 4:32).

"Forbearing one another, and forgiving one another, if any man have a quarrel against any: even as Christ forgave you, so also do ye" (Colossians 3:13).

"Looking diligently lest any man fail of the grace of God; lest any root of bitterness springing up trouble you, and thereby many be defiled," (Hebrews 12:15).

"Then came Peter to him, and said, Lord, how oft shall my brother sin against me, and I forgive him? Till seven times? Jesus saith unto him, I say not unto thee, until seven times: but, until seventy times seven" (Matthew 18:21-22).

You have to rehearse Scriptures like these in your mind and even run for your Bible if necessary.

Taking your thoughts captive requires action. Decide that you will not allow those negative thoughts to enter or stay in your mind. Through the Word of God, force your mind and your thoughts to be obedient.

There is no doubt in my mind that sometimes people willfully set out to harm you and bring you under severe persecution. There are people that are very hateful. Sometimes you find yourself hated and persecuted for no reason. The persecutor may be close to you, a friend, a relative, a church member, a spouse, your own child, and sometimes even your own pastor. You are overwhelmed by the amount of venom and hatred sent your way by people who are supposed to love and take care of you. *What do you expect me to do?* You ask. *Can I forgive these people? How do I not allow unforgiveness in when I am suffering such terrible pain?*

Love your enemies and pray for those who persecute you.

This is the commandment of God. If you love me, God says, you will keep my commandments (John 14:15).

Your love for God is also being tested. The first thing you must do when tempted to retaliate. Whenever you feel like harboring hate and unforgiveness, say, *how much do I love God? How will this affect my relationship with my God?* If you love God, you must endeavor to do as He says. Pray for those who persecute you.

Through the Eyes of the Persecutor

Do you realize that a lot of the people who are hurting and persecuting you need your prayer? A person cannot be that hateful if his heart is in right standing with God. Sometimes these people have been hurt themselve, and they are trapped in the same pain they are trying to pull you in. Satan has them captive, and they need to be freed. How are you going to free them? They can only be freed through the love of God. How are they going to see His love? God wants them to see His love through you.

Love your enemies, Jesus commands. Through you, they must see how much I love them, I do not wish for any to perish, Jesus pleads with us to love them. What are you going to do with what Jesus commands?

These people who are hurting you need your prayer. Through your prayer and intercession the Holy Spirit will be able to convict and show them Jesus and His great love towards them, and perhaps they can be changed.

These people are also Christians; you say. *They are supposed to know better.* It does not matter the label; anyone can be deceived and be held bound by unforgiveness, hatred, and coldness of heart. You have no idea sometimes the suffering of those who have wronged you. You cannot see because you are disobedient, and you refuse to do as God says...pray for them. When you pray you will see clearly through the revelation of the Holy Spirit what to pray for, and you will be shocked sometimes at the pain of your persecutor.

I once stumbled upon a page on Facebook called:

When someone says 'I love you' Just ask, 'for how long'?

Someone shared a quote from that page that says,

Seriously, life is better when you decide you don't care.

I saw the quote and immediately looked what page it was coming from. I was curious, so I clicked on the page and realized that it has over Eighty Nine Thousand likes. The name of the page, the quote, and the amount of likes told me something.

There are a lot of people hurting in our world. The numbers on this page have not even scratched the surface. When you can decide that life is better if you decide you don't care, then your heart is in a serious condition. There is no room for love in that heart. Hearts like these are obviously developed because of the hurt that was experienced. To get to a stage where you are always asking, out loud, or not, 'how long?' every time someone says to you 'I love you', shows a heart battered by brokenness and distrust. We meet these people every day. Sometimes our persecutors, and the persons that hurt us, are these very people, with this same concept, known, or unknown to them.

You deal with hurt and persecution by doing exactly what God instructs in His Word. If you have been wronged, if you are hurting, and have allowed unforgiveness to creep into your heart, go before God for forgiveness. Begin searching His Word for what He says, the answer is right there.

"Dearly beloved, avenge not yourselves, but rather give place unto wrath: for it is written, Vengeance is mine; I will repay, saith the Lord" (Romans 12:19).

"The LORD shall fight for you, and ye shall hold your peace" (Exodus 14:14).

There are times when people are just downright disobedient to God themselves and are agents of the devil. It is still not your responsibility to retaliate. Your instructions are...forgive.

"I got this," God is saying, "I will repay."

When God fights for you, you will never lose a battle. When you try to fight for yourself, you are only burying yourself further into hurt, frustration, and anger. The enemy comes in and entangles you even further into depression and sadness, and plagues you even more with thoughts of injustice. It is so much easier to turn things over to God and allow Him to fight on your behalf.

In an army, a soldier must follow strict commands, or he may lose his life. In most armies, if you are hurt the instruction is to stay down. A fellow soldier is responsible to carry you to safety. If you stay down, and the enemy captures you, then sure enough there will be a search, and troops will be sent in to rescue you. When you are hurt and persecuted the best thing to do is to follow the instructions of God, your Commander and Chief. Be silent...stay down! I have already commanded someone to help you through this and bring comfort to you. I have instructed a brother, or a sister, to come rescue you and bring you to safety. I have given angels charge over you. I am the one fighting this battle. I am in charge here, if you let me. Obey His commands for He never loses a battle. Never forget that!

CHAPTER 4

How You Know You Have Not Forgiven

"Looking diligently lest any man fail of the grace of God; lest any root of bitterness springing up trouble you, and thereby many be defiled" (Hebrews 2:15).

Unforgiveness can sometimes be subtle. You may think you have forgiven, but deep down inside you there may be hidden unforgiveness. You have to search yourself and dig to find it, especially if you have been hurt severely. It becomes dangerous when you say, "Okay I forgive her," but you have never dealt with the hurt according to the Word of God.

In Chapter nine of this book, you will clearly see the process of overcoming unforgiveness. Right now I want to show you how to identify unforgiveness. In showing you this, I must tell you a story of my own life.

It was an ordinary day. Nothing special was happening, except I had a whole 'tonne' of work to do. That included interviewing persons interested in becoming a part of the ministry I lead. Getting through all my work, and the interviews I had for that day was difficult. As always, when I have interviews I felt flustered and unprepared. I just wanted it to be over. I knew I needed help for the ministry, but conducting interviews I disliked. *Okay let's just do this!* I thought.

If I can remember correctly, this was my second interview for the day. I was looking at the credentials for the woman I was about to interview. *Why does she want to be a part of this ministry?* I thought. She already seemed to have a lot to do. She was a well accomplished individual and the Chief Executive Officer of her company, a company whose mission involves helping others. She is already paying her debt to society by her work, and therefore, by extension her debt to God. *Should I interview her?* The thoughts plagued me. I did not think I wanted this person; I did not think she would even have time for this ministry. *Interview her anyway,* was the nagging feeling I was getting. As I often respond to these feelings, I shrugged my shoulders and said "ah well!" With that, I picked up the phone and dialed. Little did I know that my life was about to be changed in ways I could never imagine.

The voice on the other end startled me. Allissa had so much cheerfulness in her voice it would cause even the saddest of persons to become joyful. As I spoke to her, my whole outlook changed. I wanted this woman on my team.

She said nothing special that lead me to believe this, it was just her personality that could not remain hidden even in a phone conversation. *A person this joyful would make an excellent addition to your team.* I thought. As we continued our conversation, Allissa expressed her desire to tell me about herself.

The experience she was about to share was nothing good. There was no happiness in that story, no joy in what she told me that day. As she related her story, I found as a woman I could identify with her struggles, though I could only imagine the amount of pain she suffered, and was still suffering. I have never gone through anything like she experienced, or even close. All my own problems seem to just pale into insignificance right there. We spoke that day like we knew each other for decades.

I know myself, and so I know that what just transpired was nowhere in my personality. I was done with my interviews for that day. I was not going to interview anyone else. I wanted to hold on to that experience. If Allissa would accept, I already knew without a second interview, or consultation I wanted her.

From our conversation, I sensed a woman who had a deep love for God, and a deep desire to serve. I had found a woman who stood in the face of adversity, not allowing anything to turn her heart from her God. She was willing to help other women overcome similar experiences. I had found someone who despite the intense pain of her experience could transfer joy over a telephone. The impact of that conversation will forever be etched in my memory. Even then, I never realized it was God who brought this woman into my life.

My Background

I was grown in a Christian home with both parents, and six siblings. I was brought up in Kingston Jamaica and still lived just outside its perimeters. Even though we were poor growing up, I did not even realize it because in my own eyes there was no family happier than mine.

In a matriarchal society like Jamaica, I am always among the few who had both parents. I felt tremendously privileged and secured. My father instilled in us the Word of God. We would rise at dawn every morning to devotion, and occasionally be called to impromptu prayer. My father is a man of prayer and the Word. There was no problem, question or situation that my father could not quickly find an answer for in God's Word. From a child, I developed a great love for God because of my parents. My mother stayed home to take care of us. I remember as a child always trying to escape the world. I loved to be home. I knew when I got home my Mom would be there waiting for me, and my dinner would be prepared. My house had so much love and laughter! People who visited would often comment that we had no need for a television, or other source of entertainment. Growing up I had enormous self confidence, and a sense of security. God and my family were my rock.

My church was equally great! I remember entering the doors of my church as a child and would be afraid to walk straight down the center aisle, especially if the service already started. There was an awe surrounding the church that told me God was there. We entered reverently, as one of our rules of conduct outlined. It was taken literally in our church. As a little girl, I always loved the worship service on a Sunday morning. The congregation sang like angels. I would close my eyes and listen, afraid to sing for fear I might miss the sound of the voices of men and angels worshipping. This was exactly how it felt. It felt and sounded as if there were a million voices of angels assisting the congregation to sing. Only something from heaven could be so beautiful!

My Pastor I adored. He was an upright man. You could see God in his eyes. He was tall and strong in stature, and he commanded your attention. He had such an authority, it felt like giving respect to him, was giving respect to God. He represented God. That is how I saw him through the eyes of a child. Needless to say, my world was one that had tremendous security. I hated the outside world; I hated school. As long as it is going to take me outside my home, and it is not church, I hated it. I felt I could only find peace at home, or when I went to church.

As I grew, these two places became my sanctuaries and places of refuge. There was not an activity at church I was not involved in, and I still managed to do extremely well at school. I always attributed it to the fact that God was with me. God became my closest friend. My church family became my true family. To make this story short, something happened that changed my life and my entire perspective. My old pastor died and left the church to youth pastor. This man was also a man whom I respected. In my younger days he taught me so much about God. Our small church must have had about one hundred young people at the time. Compared to a lot of churches in Jamaica, and for a small island, this was a lot. These young people were my closest friends; I had no friends at school, or anywhere else. I felt no need to.

It was not before long that my 'new pastor' started preaching heresy. It got to the point where he started preaching that we are gods...that's how severely heretic his massages became. The church split, the young people split, my friends split. Imagine my shock and dismay when my world fell apart. I never expected these people to behave the way they did. They were my world.

The other part of my shock came when my family was being severely persecuted by all those we knew to be our friends and brothers. We chose to stand up for God and were punished for it. I suffered so much hurt and pain it was unbelievable. Just imagine a young teenager who thought her world was so perfect, see it crumble before her eyes. Imagine a young girl despised by the only friends she knew and loved. Imagine your own pastor hating you, and wishing you harm. That's exactly what I walked through.

My heart was broken; totally crushed. My family knew adversity like never before, but my parents stood in the face of adversity and leaned on God as we leaned on them. Sometimes, I could not find God at all in the situation, so I looked to my father who was a stalwart. I learned to forgive these people, I learned to get over the hurt and the pain in time, or so I thought.

I quickly learned that the one person who would never let me go is God. I quickly learned He was the oly one worthy of my trust. Years went by, and I changed. As my perspective changed I learned to become more sociable with the 'outside world', those who were not of my church.

God finally freed our curch from that tyranny. The church administration and head of the Executive Council stepped in and took control. I could never understand why they or God allowed such atrocity to continue as long as it did. Now as an adult I understand. There were lessons I needed to learn to make me who I should be.

The Lesson God Wanted Me to Learn

As the days ensued, Allissa and I became inseparable. I quickly found that our relationship was different from what I was used to. Even though Allissa sought advice from me on many occasions, and probably thought that she was the one learning from me, there was so much I was learning from her. There was this obvious love for God, and people that flowed from her so purely. God spoke to this woman like you would speak to your friend, yet she was so humble about it and still sought advice, not wanting to make any mistake.

Through gruelling circumstances and adversities she had such deep desire to help others. In the coming days, we laughed together, cried together, prayed together, plan together. She had become my friend.

Most people in my circle when parting company would say to me,

"I love you."

Whether they meant it or not is a different story. Usually the end of a conversation would go like this,

"I love you,"

Then I would say,

"Love you too."

The next thing that followed is goodbye.

I had come to expect it from those around me; it had become a parting phrase. The difference with Allissa is when she said, "I love you," you knew she meant it. You felt the love of God exuding from her. She said it with all her heart. One day as we were about to end our conversation the usual thing happened. "I love you," she said. "I love you too," was my response.

As I hung up the phone, I realized this no longer was a parting phrase, not with Allissa. It was genuinely heart felt love between sisters. There was now a bond between us. All of a sudden I felt the need to resist it. Something was saying to me...danger! *What's going on? I didn't want this. I didn't ask for this to happen* so I went before God protesting.

"No," I said. "God I do not want this."

"Want what?" God pretended to be oblivious to what I was saying, He wanted me to explain.

"I love Allissa okay, I do, but I was not trying to find a friend when I met her," I explained.

"What's wrong with a friend? You say you have many friends, so now what's the problem?" God responded.

I did not know what the problem was; neither could I at the time explain why I felt the way I did. I felt out of control. I felt like she invaded my space and tore down an immense wall that I built over the years, but I did not want to admit it. I know God was about to win this argument so I ended it.

No matter how hard I tried in the following days, I could do nothing about the close friendship Allissa and I shared. The damage was already done.

I did not know until Allissa came into my life that I had so much unforgiveness in me. As we grew closer, it felt very strange. Nobody, but my family was ever allowed to come close to me. I had successfully built an imaginary wall around my heart. Inside these walls you had my family, which consisted of, my husband and kids, my mother and father, my siblings and their spouses, and other close in laws. Directly outside its parameters were those I labelled friends. These were the people whom I would say "I love you" to at the end of a conversation and felt that I meant it. These were the people I allowed to come so close to this wall I had built, but they could never pass it. This imaginary wall was there to guard my heart against hurt. Directly behind those people, were the people I attended church with, or were somewhat closely associated with. Then there was everybody else. I had a totally controlled system in operation.

I wanted to minister to people. I had a passion for helping women and seeing people saved. I got up every morning at the dawn of the day, even though sometimes I did not feel like it, and wrote devotionals so that someone could read and hear about the love of God. I had devoted my life to serve. I counted it an honor that God chose me to serve His people. So now what was the problem? I love people!

Later I found out that what I called love was not the love God wanted me to give. God was saying, there is a lesson you need to learn; you have allowed unforgiveness to place a wall around your heart no one could get pass. That is not how I want you to live. This is not my plan for you.

Allissa always says to me,

"God sent you to me."

I would say in response to her,

"You have no idea...God sent you to me."

I knew she had no idea of what I spoke, but I was in such a state that God knew He had to send someone like her to me. Even when Allissa was crying she was laughing. She would cry this second, and the next second she was laughing. It was weird how she still had joy although she was being hurt by those who should be protecting her. Somehow, with her always bubbling personality, and her tone of voice being a constant exclamation, she managed to break through that imaginary wall. That wall I had unknowingly constructed to guard my heart. Now I did not know what to do. I kept protesting to God and to myself until one day I decided to give up. Now Allissa breached that wall, and I wanted her to stay. I no longer wanted to keep her at bay, and so I went to God.

"God this is your fault,' I said. 'I know you did this on purpose, and so now you are going to have to take the blame. If she hurts me, you are to be blamed."

I left at that because I never wanted to hear what God had to say on the matter. I was too afraid, but God was determined to teach me a lesson.

I also knew that Allissa was a part of my life for much more than the present lesson God was trying to teach me. God probably had a million reasons why He brought us together. We had the same heart, and the same desire to serve and help others, but right now God was using her to be a part of what He wanted to show me. I wasn't willing to admit what I was feeling. I wasn't willing to admit that I had shut people out of my life for a long time. I pushed every feeling I had to the back of my head. I couldn't understand, so I left it there. God was about to show me that I had to admit to my wrong and deal with it.

It was again an ordinary morning and I woke up feeling good. As usual I went straight to prayer and devotion to God. As I was closing my prayer, there was this uneasy feeling in me. The thought came to me to pray some more. I brushed it aside; it was breakfast time for my family. I got off my knees. Shortly after, I was in the kitchen. What happened next would be a shock to both me and my husband.

My husband and I had a simple difference of
opinion; we got into a fight which left us both
sitting down in serious retrospect. Neither of us
could understand how we got so angry at the other.
I brought things up that happened in the first year of
our marriage, so many years ago.

Be diligent, the Bible says, *lest the root of bitterness
springs up and trouble you.*

I had not been diligent. I had allowed bitterness in
my heart so much that now it was troubling me, and
those around me too, those that I held dear and
loved. The Bible says, many can become defiled by
the bitterness in us. This was exactly what was
happening to me. I did not even know my state. I
never realized. My lesson was not yet done.

The next time Allissa and I spoke, we found
ourselves talking about past hurts and how deeply
people had hurt us. I found that as I spoke to her
about a friend that had hurt me years ago, tears
welled up in my eyes, and my heart was breaking.
There are things that I never spoke about to anyone
else that I spoke about with Allissa. Of course, I
only skimmed the surface because I didn't know
how to trust. What a state to be in. So deep was my
pain I could not even open up to someone about it. I
felt it was tearing me apart. I didn't want to fall
apart as it made me feel vulnerable. I was exhausted
when I finished that conversation. It caused me to
remember not only that friend I told her about, but
all the past hurts that I had experienced. I

remembered all that happened to me as a child at my church. Everything that anyone had ever done to me, I remembered in those few hours. I was ready for bed. Like most times when I find something worrying I would go to God, and then to sleep, and that I did.

Unforgiveness is a terrible state to be in, it is even worst when you think you have forgiven, and you have not.

"Therefore, as *the* elect of God, holy and beloved, put on tender mercies, kindness, humility, meekness, longsuffering; bearing with one another, and forgiving one another, if anyone has a complaint against another; even as Christ forgave you, so you also must do" (Colossians 3:12-13).

As the Lord forgives; not as we deem forgiveness to be! God makes Himself vulnerable again each time we hurt Him. Each time we come to Him saying we are sorry, He accepts us again. I am not naive; I know that there are some people who are not supposed to be a part of our life. However, it should never be a heart of unforgiveness that pushes them away.

The next day, after Allissa and I had that conversation about past hurts, I had a funeral to attend. On my way to the funeral, my husband and I picked up my sister-in-law so we could attend the funeral together. She handed me a book called, The Bait of Satan, to read. In this book, it was talking about how to prevent being offended. As I read the book, God continued to speak to my heart.

What do you want from me God? I genuinely wanted to know.

Seeing I already set myself to obey His every command, I decided that whatever He wanted I would do. I told God as I read,

"I will do as you say."

"Okay," God said, "I want you to tear down that wall of unforgiveness you have built inside your heart. You have unknowingly locked people out of your heart for so long because you did not forgive those people that wronged you so many years ago."

I protested, "I forgave them."

"Really?" God said, "What happened with Allissa?"

"I don't know," I admitted, "It's weird! It's as if there is a tearing, and someone who was not supposed to, had gotten past the inner circle of my heart." I said.

"Don't you find it strange that you could not explain the tearing as Allissa got closer to you?" God asked.

"Yes, it felt strange, and it felt like a massive invasion." I responded.

"When you finally submitted, what did it feel like?"
God asked.

"Good!" I replied,

"But now I'm scared so now what?" I wanted to
know.

I remembered at that moment a section of the book,
The Bait of Satan, I was reading. It said that I
should love expecting nothing in return. *Really!* I
thought. The author, John Bevere, explained that
when you have friends, or relationships, you should
give your all but not expect anything in return. Any
return you get is a blessing and not an expectation.
This way you will not be disappointed when
someone does not meet your expectations. Since
Allissa was the topic of discussion, I addressed
God.

"Are you trying to tell me that I should expect
nothing from Allissa and her friendship and that
whatever I get from our friendship is a blessing and
should not be an expectation?"

"And more than that," was God's reply, "If she
hurts you, you should be ready and willing to
forgive her, and keep her in the same position where
she now stands in your heart. This is called
unconditional love. This love is what I have for
you." God said.

I understood clearly. This was not about whether Allissa would hurt me. This was about God saying to me; your love should have no condition. There was an instant freeing feeling and my fear disappeared. I don't have to live wondering if someone is going to hurt me because I should be prepared to love them no matter what.

People cannot meet our high expectations all the time. What makes us, faulty humans, demand so much from each other? People are bound to make mistakes and be foolish, and yes, sometimes may even hurt us. God loves us no matter what. We have hurt Him so many times by our actions and rejection, yet He loves us anyway and forgives us freely.

As God continued to speak to my heart, I recognized the position I was in, and it was ugly. God then began to show me that even those that I claimed to have within the walls of the inner circle of my heart, I could not forgive.

"You argued with your husband, and you were able to remember clearly what he did to you so long ago," God said, "Not only one incident but many."

As I argued with my husband that day and brought up some of the wrongs I thought he did, it felt like he did them yesterday. These things happened years ago, no one should be able to remember the accounts so plainly. It was clear to me that I had not forgiven him.

As I knelt on my knees that night God showed me my state so clearly.

"As a child you were hurt by people whom you thought you could trust. Since then you have found it hard to allow people near your heart. Even those whom you thought you were willing to open your heart to, like your husband and your family, are being affected by your unforgiveness. You had your defenses up just in case. You were not aware of this, but now you must repent."

Allisa and that argument with my husband were the instruments God used to show me my heart. Buried deep inside me was unforgiveness. The root of bitterness was in me, and I needed to get it out. I cried to God, and asked Him in that moment for His forgiveness, and I prayed for those who persecuted me. I was free! I felt in that moment a freeness I could not explain. I was no longer afraid to allow people near me, or love them purely, or let them into my heart. Unforgiveness was exposed and dealt with and I was ready. As I knelt there just me and God being happy in the moment, I knew I had to write this down for someone else. I knew my experience was not only for me, but to teach someone else the same lessons I had learned.

Are you shielding your heart because you have been hurt? Do you remember past things that people have done to you years ago as if it were yesterday? Do you get hurt again every time you remember, or speak about it? Do you find yourself still angry at the person when the memory of the past comes to you? My friend, you may think you have, but you have not forgiven.

CHAPTER 5

Unforgiveness Holds You Bound

"Therefore the kingdom of heaven is like a certain king who wanted to settle accounts with his servants. And when he had begun to settle accounts, one was brought to him who owed him ten thousand talents. But as he was not able to pay, his master commanded that he be sold, with his wife and children and all that he had, and that payment be made. The servant therefore fell down before him, saying, 'Master, have patience with me, and I will pay you all.' Then the master of that servant was moved with compassion, released him, and forgave him the debt. "But that servant went out and found one of his fellow servants who owed him a hundred denarii; and he laid hands on him and took *him* by the throat, saying, 'Pay me what you owe!' So his fellow servant fell down at his feet and begged him, saying, 'Have patience with me, and I will pay you all.' And he would not, but went and threw him into prison till he should pay the debt. So when his fellow servants saw what had been done, they were very grieved, and came and told their master all that had been done. Then his master, after he had called him, said to him, 'You wicked servant! I forgave you all that debt because you begged me. Should you not also have had compassion on your fellow servant, just as I had pity on you?' And his master was angry, and delivered him to the torturers until he should pay all that was due to him. "So My heavenly Father also will do to you if each of you, from his heart, does not forgive his brother his trespasses" (Matthew 18:23-35).

Do you notice in the passage above that the man that was not willing to forgive owed such a huge debt in comparison to the person who owed him? The same holds true with us and God. We cannot pay the debt we owe to Him, yet He is willing to forgive us time and time again. The hurt that others inflict on us is nothing compared to how much we constantly hurt, fail, and turn our backs on God. Jesus in the parable said, "You wicked servant, I forgave all your debts, shouldn't you also have the same compassion on your fellow servant?"

What happens next is frightening. The Lord of that servant delivered him to the torturers. Jesus said, "Your heavenly Father will do the same thing to you if you do not forgive." I did not say it; Jesus did. Is He lying? No, He is not. As it relates to us today, the torturers are the devil and his angels. It is dangerous to harbor unforgiveness in your heart.

Can you imagine going to God asking for forgiveness and He responds by saying, "No." Imagine how startled you would be at such an answer. Most of us believe that a loving God would never say that. "Oh, God will not turn me away," you say.

"For if you forgive men their trespasses, your heavenly Father will also forgive you. But if you do not forgive men their trespasses, neither will your

Father forgive your trespasses." (Matthew 6:14-15).

If you do not forgive, your heavenly Father will not forgive you. It is laid out so plainly in the Scriptures, yet we still stumble at it. How often do we ask the forgiveness of God? I know that I do plenty. Sometimes I just cannot be sure if I have sinned. I may have said the wrong thing and offended someone, or done something without knowing. At times, I do something that I know about, am sorry and need God's forgiveness. No matter how repentant you are, or how many tears you cry, God's answer remains the same for an unforgiving heart.

Go and forgive your brother or I will not forgive you.

Getting up off your knees thinking that you are alright, and you have been forgiven, does not mean you are. Your opinion in the matter does not matter. What is written in God's Word is what counts. What matters is the countless times He says to us in His Word... forgive.

Unforgiveness holds us bound. There cannot be a total freeing until it is rooted from our hearts.

"Follow peace with all men, and holiness, without which no man shall see the Lord," (Hebrews 12:14).

If you have unforgiveness in your heart, you have not yet attained holiness. Holiness is a requirement to see God. Unforgiveness is a trap of Satan. He will make you feel as if you are justified in what you are doing. Hurting can be so painful that it feels like you are doing the right thing to keep those who wronged you at bay. Oftentimes, those that love you are victims of your unforgiving heart. They cannot make the slightest mistake around you. You judge them based on what someone else has done to you. You are trapped in this continual, damning cycle of unforgiveness.

"And Abram said unto Lot, let there be no strife, I pray thee, between me and thee, and between my herdsmen and thy herdsmen; for we be brethren. Is not the whole land before thee? Separate thyself, I pray thee, from me: if thou wilt take the left hand, then I will go to the right; or if thou depart to the right hand, then I will go to the left," (Genesis 13:8-9).

God was blessing Abram, and he was increasing in wealth. His nephew Lot was also blessed. They were so blessed that the land could not contain both their cattle. Their servants began to strive. Surely this situation could have gone a different way, but Abraham strove for peace. 'I do not want any strife or contention," he said. "Choose where you want to go, and let us part ways. Wherever you go, I'll go in the opposite direction," Abram said to Lot. Of course, Lot chose the best plains. Abraham could have harbored resentment. He could have said, "I am the one who took you here and made you rich. I should be the one allowed to choose where I want to go." He could have resented Lot for choosing the best plain, but he chose to part in peace.

My point is, sometimes it is necessary for a separation of ways in order that there be peace. God will show you in all wisdom what to do. However, there should never be a parting with unforgiveness in your heart. Abraham loved Lot none the less, even though he was selfish, and his herdsmen were causing trouble. It was Abram who interceded on Lot's behalf, and God rescued him and his family from Sodom and Gomorrah.

If you have found yourself in a situation where there is a parting of ways. Do not allow this to cause you to be resentful and unforgiving. Separation, for whatever reason, does not give you the right to hate. Forgiveness does not necessarily mean closeness. Forgiveness means that your heart is pure towards the individual who wronged you, and you love them with an unconditional love.

If you have found yourself in a situation where strife or anything else has caused a separation, ask yourself, "Can I truly still intercede for that person, even though I may have been persecuted by them? Can I pray for them? If I see them, what would my reactions be?" Abram could pray for Lot, and he could embrace him in love the next time they met. If you cannot do that, then unforgiveness has its hold on you.

Unforgiveness Hinders Your Faith and Keeps you from the Abundant Life

"Therefore I say unto you, what things soever ye desire, when ye pray, believe that ye receive them, and ye shall have them. And when ye stand praying, forgive, if ye have ought against any: that your Father also which is in heaven may forgive you your trespasses" (Mark 11:24-25).

Jesus was teaching a very important lesson about mustard seed faith. He was teaching that faith can remove mountains no matter how small that faith is.

"Anything you desire you can pray and believe that you have it and you will," Jesus taught.

I noticed something in these verses that hit home to me. Jesus said,

"When you pray believe that you receive."

Then Jesus was quick to point out, "However, when you pray forgive so that you can get forgiveness."

Do you yet see where I am going with this? Unforgiveness stands in the way of your answer and prevent your faith from coming into operation. You can remove mountains if you have faith, believe and pray, but while praying ensure you forgive so that you can be forgiven. Why? If you have iniquity in your heart, the Lord will not hear you (Psalm 66:18). It is through the power of God by faith that you can move mountains. So God has to hear your prayer of faith before anything can happen. If unforgiveness is in your heart, it is now standing in the way of your blessing. You cannot move forward; you are being held bound by this sin. You cannot remove mountains with an unforgiving heart.

"...I am come that they might have life, and that they might have it more abundantly" (John 10:10).

This abundant life that God promises is a life of fullness, fullness of joy, hope, peace blessings, and fullness in every area of your life. The abundant life starts here on earth, It allows you to ask what you will and receive it (John 14:13), It allows you to tread upon serpents and scorpions (Luke 10:19), it allows you to be victorious over the enemy (1 Corinthians 15:57). Abundant life allows you full privilege as a son or daughter of God (Romans 8:17). Unforgiveness is a sin and all sin separates you from God. Sin robs you of your privileges of sonship. Sin prevents you from standing in the presence of God. Let me explain.

"But your iniquities have separated between you and your God, and your sins have hid his face from you, that he will not hear." Isaiah 59:2.

A Holy God shuns the presence of sin. When I go before God, I pray to be cleansed from sin whether I am aware that I have sinned or not. I ask because I want to ensure that the Lord hears me. I am aware that I embodied in a sinful flesh, so I am careful to ask for cleansing by the blood of Jesus at all times. I am also conscious that my sin will block me from entering God's presence. Sin will make Him hide His face from me. He hides His face because He is a Holy God and to a righteous God, sin is ugly. Unforgiveness will separate you from God. If you are separated from God where is your privilege as a son? You cannot ask what you will and receive it, if He is not hearing you. You cannot enter boldly before the throne room of God with sin. You cannot have victory over the enemy with sin in your life. There goes your abundant life! It is God who gives fullness of life. This overflowing of joy, peace, blessings, and prosperity can only come from Him. If you allow sin to take root in your heart, then you will not live in this abundance that Jesus came so you can have.

The Scripture says, "The thief cometh not, but for to steal, and to kill, and to destroy" (John 10:10).

The devil will steal your abundant life of joy, peace, health, and happiness, and all that comes with abundance, if you allow sin to dwell in you. The devil knows that the only way he can destroy you is to make you remain in sin. He has succesfully fed people with many reasons why they should remain in unforgiveness. He has hidden the truth about it from the eyes of many. The devil has allowed many to believe that they have forgiven, when they have not.

When I first started in ministry, I was startled by the amount of people who were ill. So great was my distress that I decided to write about the healing power of Jesus. Alot of these sicknesses stemmed from emotional reasons. As I looked closer at unforgiveness, I could not help but wonder if many people would not be made whole if they forgave.

Studies show that anger and bitterness caused by unforgiveness can affect your health. Anger and bitterness can throw your body in a state of stress. Some studies believe that even blood flow to your heart and joint can be restricted by this tension. Your breathing can become difficult, and your immune system can become impaired. Of course, you might guess that your unforgiving heart can lead to heart attack, and many other chronic illnesses. The researches have turned up lists of diseases that are the result of unforgiveness. You can do a research yourself into this. The point I am trying to make is unforgiveness can ruin even your physical body. We need to carefully assess our hearts. This dangerous sin can cause death, not only to your spirit, but also to your body. I suggest to you that you cannot live by faith or in abundance if you have not forgiven.

Forgiving yourself is Also Important

Some people are held in chains of unforgiveness of themselves. We become so judgmental that we find it hard to forgive even ourselves. My father once said to me when I found myself in that state of unforgiveness of self,

"There is not a just man upon earth."

We beat our self up with the question, "How could I have done that."

How?

Because there is none good but the Father (Mark 10:18). We are all born in sin and shaped in iniquity (Psalm 51:5). We have inherited Adam's nature. Sin can be cleansed by the blood of Jesus only. We of ourselves can do nothing right. We have the righteousness of God and our own righteousness is like filthy rags (Isaiah 64:6). It is only by God's undeserved favor (grace) that we are saved (Ephesians 2:8-9). We are going to slip up, and we are going to make mistakes. No matter how great the sin, the blood of Jesus cleanses from all sin (1 John1:7). The important thing to remember when you sin is that you must repent. A broken and contrite heart, God will not turn away (Psalm 51:17).

The devil will want to bombard you with your sin. He will even use other people in your life to constantly remind you. God shows His love for us, in that while we were yet sinners Christ died (Romans 5:8). All of us were sinners, one big bundle of sinners. No one can condemn you because it is Christ that died for you (Roman 8:34).

Satan cannot even talk to you because there is no redemption for him. He knows that he is condemned and he wants you to feel that way too. Stop beating yourself up! So what if someone else knows? So what if you feel disgraced? Sin is going to make you feel disgrace; it is a reproach. All sin is a reproach and all are disgraced by sin. The good news is Jesus Christ takes away our sin and removes the disgrace if we allow Him.

Proverbs 6:16 says,

"Six things do the Lord hate: seven are an abomination to Him."

When you examine the seven sins listed, it includes some of the sins that most people refer to as minor.

A proud look and a lying tongue

There are those of us who are so proud and we lie so often yet we think nothing of it.

Those that sow discord among friends.

There are still some of us who may not lie so much and might not be as proud but we gossip and turn friends against each other but we think nothing of it.

What am I saying? If you have committed any sin at all, those that we deem small or great, we are able to get forgiveness from God. We often stumble over what we call 'great sins', yet the 'little sins' are so hateful to God. The 'great sins' are the ones that we cannot forgive ourselves for. In God's eyes the 'little sins' are also hateful, but He forgives us for them all if we repent. If a Holy God can forgive us, then we can forgive ourselves, no matter how small or great the sin is.

One of the reasons we cannot forgive ourselves is because of pride. How ironic! The sin that Proverbs pointed out that God hates. Do you see how deceptive Satan is, and how he holds us bound? We cannot forgive ourselves because our pride says we have committed an unforgivable sin. Now we are trapped in the sin of unforgiveness and also the sin of pride. That is not very smart, is it? You need to let go. Ask God to forgive you and forgive yourself.

CHAPTER 6

Love Covers a Multitude of Sin

"Love suffers long and is kind; love does not envy; love does not parade itself, is not puffed up; does not behave rudely, does not seek its own, is not provoked, thinks no evil; does not rejoice in iniquity, but rejoices in the truth; bears all things, believes all things, hopes all things, endures all things. Love never fails." (1 Corinthians 13:4-8).

Every time I read, quote, or think of this Scripture I feel grossly inadequate. My ability to love comes into question, and I suspect I fall terribly short in many instances. Unless you have the love of God in your heart, unless your heart is totally transformed and your mind renewed, unless your will is in total submission to God and you are in total obedience to His commands, you cannot do what this Scripture says.

Let's dissect a little bit. *Love suffers long.* How long have you been suffering with those who are hurting or persecuting you? We get so easily offended, and are so quickly willing to throw away relationships. Sometimes we even complain that we are suffering too long. How long did Jesus suffer with man? He died over two thousand years ago, and man still rejects Him today. How long is Jesus willing to suffer with you? A lifetime! You keep hurting and failing Him over and over again, and He keeps allowing you to do so and forgives you.

Love is kind. Showing kindness to those who have offended or hurt you is one of the hardest things to do. This is a true test of our love. Let's think about this! Your enemy cannot hurt you. Most times, those who are able to hurt you are those closest to you. Those you say you love. Do you think that the Scripture, when it says love is kind, means kind only in some circumstances? Love is kind all the time, even when she is hurting. Kindness is an action, but it must first start in the heart. Sometimes we do kind acts, but we are not doing it from the heart? We may be doing it to be boastful, or to prove to ourselves that we can be kind even though we are hurting. We may be doing it out of duty. None of this reflects love. Kindness must be a genuine state of the heart.

Love does not envy. This is an entirely different book, but let me attempt to put it into perspective in this context with an example. Ann has a disagreement with her close friend. There is hurt which was not dealt with thus leading to unforgiveness. Ann and her friend drift apart. They still remain in the same immediate surrounding, like at church, or work. Suddenly Ann feels the need to compete with her friend. When they were friends, her friend could do nothing wrong. She encouraged and supported her. Now there is a fall out, Ann wants nothing good for her friend anymore. She wants her to hurt and suffer as much as she is hurting. If the opposite happens, Ann gets envious.

You must be careful that even if the person that hurt you is excelling above you there is no envy. Alot of times, envy is a product of unforgiveness. If you allow yourself to begin to envy your friend because your friend excels, I put the argument forward to you, you never loved your friend. Am I being harsh? No, this is just an attempt to reveal to you your state so you can change. Love does not envy.

Does not parade itself, is not puffed up, does not behave itself rudely or inappropriately. Your spouse and you had a quarrel. You have been hurt by his words and actions. All this transpired when you were about to go out to dinner with company. It is an important event for him. Maybe he is taking you to a work event where his boss and all his co-workers will be. All the way there you are fuming in your heart. *How could he have done that, how could he have said that to me?* When you finally get there everyone knows, by your actions and expressions, that you both had a quarrel. You behave yourself inappropriately, and you embarrass the person you claim to love. All because you could not put aside what happened earlier and forgive.

This is just a mild example of how our hearts can be when we hurt. Think of your own examples for all the time that you became puffed up and behaved inappropriately. For all the times you allowed unforgiveness to cause you to forget love.

Love seeks not her own, is not easily provoked. Alot of times when we are hurt it is because our own selfish desires are not fulfilled. We expect, and even demand too much from the person we say we love. When our expectations are not met, then we begin to feel hurt. Our relationships are based on self gratification and not love. The moment we believe our loved ones and friends can no longer do for us what we expected; we are willing to sever ties. We as humans have fallen so short of love. Love is not easily provoked, so how is it that we get provoked so easily and offended by those whom we say we love? You are not always selfish to want something of your loved one, especially when it should be given. There are times when we rightly feel that we are not treated kindly enough, with sufficient care, or even with love. However, love does not seek her own, so love will back off and give of herself.

Alot of marriages end because we fail to practice this aspect of love. Over the twelve years that I have been married, I have discovered that men are indeed from Mars and women from Venus. This makes us automatically of a different nature, and we speak an entirely different language. I have learned that when we are having a conversation, sometimes I must have a translator. That translator has to be the Holy Spirit. His only instruction may be to be kind, give up your rights. Even though you are right and you deserve what you are seeking, allow love to prevail. Very often I find that the Translator is right. When we are both calm and look at the situation again, my husband did not say, or acted as I thought, and I did not say, or acted as he thought. Our difference in citizenship and language only had us confused.

Love thinks no evil, rejoices not in iniquity, but rejoices in the truth. How often does our unforgiveness and lack of love cause us to think evil and rejoice when we hear that someone, whom we think has wronged us, fall? We even go a step further to walk and malign the person who have wronged us, and cause other persons to see them in a bad way. We devise all sorts of mischief in our hearts, and when we become successful in carrying out our evil desires, we rejoice. Let us not do this. Let us rather think no evil of those who has wronged us and forgive them. Let us rejoice in the truth. What is the truth? In this case, the truth is that forgiveness sets you free. When you have forgiven those that have hurt you, you have both set yourself free from bondage and have also set them free. Yes, that is right, **set them free**. The Bible says if you hate your brother you are a murderer (1 John 3:15). Hate and unforgiveness are what causes you to devise evil against someone and bring them into the bondage of your hate.

Love bears all things, believes all things, endures all things. Now, I had to really pause here even now that I am writing it. This is the part that every person has to depend only on the strength of God to do. In fact, we cannot love without Him. Love as described in 1Corinthians 13 can only be given by God.

Do you remember in chapter four when I said that God spoke to me regarding my friend Allissa? God said, "If she hurts you, you should be ready and willing to forgive her and keep her in the same position where she now stands in your heart. This is called unconditional love. This love is what I have for you."

I brought this up again in an attempt to explain to you what God meant by,

'Keep her in the same position where she now stands in your heart.'

How can someone hurt you, turn their backs on you, betray you, and you still love them the same way? This is exactly how God loves. Think about it. Think about from the day Adam fell in the Garden of Eden, how determined God was to restore mankind. Think about all the times that the children of Isreal provoked Him in the desert, yet He loved them and restored them, and brought them to the land He promised Abraham. Think about your own self. I am embarrassed to think about my own self and how many times I fail God, yet He rescues me, forgives me, and loves me still.

Do you think that God shifts the position that we hold in His heart every time we hurt Him? By now, we would have no place in His heart at all. He loves us the same. He does not push us away even though we break His heart and leave Him devastated at times. There are times when God allows us to bear punishment much like we do to our own children. Sometimes when we punish our children it hurts us more than it hurts them, but we do it anyway for their good. We do it because we love them. God never changes the way He feels about us.

Most marriages that end in divorce leave all involved with so much hate and resentment, in particular the divorced. Each blames the other. Oftentimes, none is willing to forgive. The love we have for others is not willing to bear all things. That is why there are so many divorces in the first place. I must hasten to say, there are times that wisdom allows us to separate from the ones we love. Sometimes you find yourself in an abusive relationship and separation becomes the only choice. Not in all instances does it mean that forgiveness does not still require a separation, as I said before. Sometimes, such separation brings about such hurt and pain. The wounds received in our experiences, in particular in broken marriages, are very deep. However, the condition of your heart must not change towards that person. You must still love and forgive. How can I love such a person? How can I love someone who has inflicted so much hurt and pain in my heart? **You cannot!** Only the love of God can bear and endure all things and still remain unchanged. Therefore, you must allow God to give you His love. You must give a heart that has suffered such tremendous hurt to God, and ask Him to allow you to love as He loves. When someone turns his back on God, when a child of God has backslidden and chooses to separate himself from God, even though God can do nothing about his choice and a separation must take place, God still loves him. The state of his heart and how much he has hurt God does not change the love of God for Him.

Unforgiveness thrives because hurt is often inflicted by those closest to us. There are mothers who have become so hateful towards their own children because they are disappointed. David cried out in 2 Samuel 18:33,

"Absolom my son, I wished I had died instead of you."

David was mourning a son who sought his life. This son, Absolom had cunningly sought to turn the hearts of the people of Judah from David, and successfully did so. He was preparing to forcefully overthrow David his father and take over his kingdom; he was his father's worst enemy. David and his men had to be on the run from Absolom because he now had a massive following who hunted David. David had to flee his palace and the security of his home. He had to run from his throne and give up his exalted position as king in order to escape the wrath of his son. David sought with all his might to preserve Absolom's life at the expense of his own. Absolom was killed unknown to him by one of his trusted soldiers. David's grief was so great when he heard the news. He wished it was he who had died instead of his son, and he went into mourning.

God said of David,

"Your heart is like mine."

I can understand why God could say that. I am sure the account I gave is not the only reason, but it is certainly one of the reasons God described David in this manner. David's love for his son could have easily turned, and he could have been unforgiving and cruel and ordered him dead a long time ago. He chose, however, to forgive and love him still. This is a love that bore and endured all things.

Friends hate each other because of hurt feelings. Brothers hate brothers, as Esau hated Jacob in Genesis 27:41, and wish them dead. The world is filled with people who walk around with unforgiveness, and are held bound because they are clueless about true love. They know nothing of the love of God.

Love bears all things and so Jesus Christ who is love chose to die a gruesome death on the cross for us. He condescended into a finite body and became man. He further subjected Himself to being spat on and mocked. Even though He could call legions of angels to help Him, love allowed Him to bear it. Isaiah 52:14 says,

"His form or body was marred or disfigured more than any other man."

The beating Jesus suffered transformed His features so that He was unrecognizable. As His hands were outstretched on the cross, as He bled and hung there by large nails that pierced through the middle of his hands, He pleaded,

"Father forgive them."

He had already forgiven. Jesus' heart of love harbored no hurt, no resentment, and no hate. He wanted to make sure that His Father forgave his killers too, and not turn His wrath towards them. He knew His father must have been hurting as He watched.

"Father forgive them, they have no idea what they are doing. They do not know I am God. Please do not hold it against them...forgive them," He cried.

Love bears all things! Have you yet hung on a cross for the one you say you love and now refuse to forgive?

Love believes all things, so as Jesus hung on that cross, He believed that those people who had asked for Him to be crucified, and even those that literally drove the nails in His hands could experience salvation. He looked down through the ages and believed that this sinful generation can turn to Him as a result of Him dying there. He saw me, and believed that I could experience salvation and be changed. He believed because He loves me.

Do you see any good in those who are hurting you? Do you recognize a soul that needs salvation? Do you see a heart crying out for help as you look at your offenders? What do you believe? Love believes all things, even when that thing seems impossible, love believes that it is.

Love never fail. Even if you are held by the strongest of cord, rope, or cable, while in midair halfway down a cliff, you may panic, believing what holds you may break, and you may fall. Love cannot break. It extends itself and reaches out at all times. It holds you when you are falling. **Love's support is unbreakable.** As love's support has to be strong because it must remain unbreakable, it cannot hold a grudge or be offended. Holding a grudge and being offended are attributes of weakness, and love must be strong. How often do we let go and give up on those we say we love. Think about your life and all those were, or those who are still in it. Have you loved, or is your love merely a conditional one?

When you love as God loves, no matter what the other person has done, you will never hold a grudge. You will never hold unforgiveness for them in your heart. The person who has hurt you will still hold the same position in your heart. You will love them the same way as you did before. You will find that as you ask God for His unconditional love, you will not be as easily hurt or offended. You will be more equipped to bear all things, endure all things, and believe all things. You may think this impossible, but rather, when you love like this life becomes so much simpler.

Do you see a hurt Jesus on the cross, or do you see someone filled with love? Love bars you from offenses and hurt.

"It doesn't matter, it really doesn't matter what they do. I love them anyway," is Jesus' approach.

What a freeing way to love! Unscathed, and unentangled by unforgiveness and bitterness of the heart!

The Bible says that love covers a multitude of sin (1 Peter 4:8). When you love like this, offenses will become sometime unrecognizable or minute. Have you ever noticed the love of a mother for a child? No matter what my children do, or how terrible the act, my love for them remains. Even if I know it deserves punishment, I punish with pain in my heart only because I know it is good for them. Sometimes, behind closed doors there are tears in my eyes, for the punishment I had to give. There is nothing that they could do that would even shift my heart, or the love I have for them.

Love is freeing; unforgiveness holds you bound. Choose rather to love.

CHAPTER 7

Unforgiveness Destroys Unity

"Now I beseech you, brethren, by the name of our Lord Jesus Christ, that ye all speak the same thing, and that there be no divisions among you; but that ye be perfectly joined together in the same mind and in the same judgment" (1 Corinthians 1:10).

Being perfectly joined together has no room for unforgiveness. You cannot be totally united in the heart with your brother if you have not forgiven him. Division and disunity has severely affected the church.There is a million reasons why, but sure enough listed among the top ones is unforgiveness. When we are not in unity, God's principles of agreement cannot take effect and so our prayers will be hindered.

"Again I say unto you, that if two of you shall agree on earth as touching anything that they shall ask, it shall be done for them of my Father which is in heaven. For where two or three are gathered together in my name, there am I in the midst of them" (Matthew 18:19-20).

We love to quote this Scripture, especially when we gather to pray. However, what we often forget is the word 'agree' in this Scripture. Agreement is not just words spoken, but it is the unity of the heart and spirit. There is a condition in this Scripture that is so often overlooked - *if two shall agree*. There are prayer meetings going on right now all over this world. Christians gather together so often to pray. We go to each others home, call each other on the phone, holds fasts and weeks of prayer. Why then is the church, not more powerful? Why are we not seeing signs and wonders as in the days of the apostles? **There is no agreement.** This disagreement stems from many reasons, but again, unforgiveness is right up there among the top things on the list. Can you imagine a church gathering to pray with brothers and sisters who have not forgiven each other in the midst? What do you expect to happen there? I can tell you - nothing! The principle of God demands agreement.

"And when the day of Pentecost was fully come, they were all with one accord in one place. And suddenly there came a sound from heaven as of a rushing mighty wind, and it filled all the house where they were sitting. And there appeared unto them cloven tongues like as of fire, and it sat upon each of them. And they were all filled with the Holy Ghost, and began to speak with other tongues, as the Spirit gave them utterance" (Acts 2:1-4).

The Holy Spirit was given to the believers when they were all in one accord - total agreement. As recorded in the Bible, the Apostles achieved great miracles, signs and many souls being saved, when they were united. When Peter and John were about to heal the lame man in Acts 3:4, they declared "look on us." A miracle was performed because they were in total agreement. I dare to put to you that the church lacks power today because of unforgiveness. Unforgiveness is one of the root sources of disunity among us.

Let's imagine a typical church. The pastor has decided that the congregation should fast and pray for something specific. The week of fasting and prayer is called, and special nights or days of prayers are organized. In that gathering, there is Peter, who cannot forgive John because he has married the woman whom he loved. There is Susan, who is mad at Jane for telling Mary what she told her in confidence. There is Pat, who does not speak to Betty because she heard she was discussing her behind her back, and so on. There is no agreement in that prayer meeting already. Then there is the pastor, who is hated by many of his members for various reasons. He is trying desperately in that prayer meeting to get some answers from God, except God is not accepting his gift because his brother in the congregation has not forgiven him and he knows. Here you have a church wasting two hours or more in a prayer meeting where nothing will happen. Unfortunately, this situation described is in many, many churches. I dare say most.

All over the Bible unity is stressed.

"That there should be no schism in the body; but that the **members should have the same care one for another**. And whether one member suffer, all the members suffer with it; or one member be honored, all the members rejoice with it" (1 Corinthians 12:25-26).

"I therefore, the prisoner of the Lord, beseech you that ye walk worthy of the vocation wherewith ye are called, With all lowliness and meekness, with long-suffering, forbearing one another in love; **endeavoring to keep the unity of the Spirit in the bond of peace**" (Ephesians 4:1-3).

"If there be therefore any consolation in Christ, if any comfort of love, if any fellowship of the Spirit, if any bowels and mercies, Fulfill ye my joy, that ye be like-minded, **having the same love, being of one accord, of one mind**. Let nothing be done through strife or vainglory; but in lowliness of mind let each esteem other better than themselves" (Philippians 2:1-3).

Where is our bowel of mercy for our brother? We are so easily offended by the things our brother does or says. In order to achieve anything as a body, we must be united. We must be in agreement. We have to put away striving which often result in unforgiveness. Each esteeming the other better than themselves is what Peter encouraged in the Word of God. It means that we prefer each other; we love each other so much that we will seek to have peace and not strife.

Unforgiveness is also the root source of hindered blessing in marriages. This is because of the same principle. There is no agreement. When a husband

and wife are in total agreement and come together in prayer, their prayers become effective because of the principle of agreement. The Bible says if two can agree, anything you ask of the Father will be done. The Bible also exhorts the wife to be submissive to her husband (1 Peter 3:1). She must follow his guidance and headship. The husband must honor his wife and recognize that he and his wife are heirs together of the grace of life. The husband must come to this realization of togetherness so that 'his prayers are not hindered,' the Bible stated in 1 Peter 3:7. When the husband and wife are in God's perfect order, there will be perfect unity between them, and their prayers will not be hindered. Being united before God is very important. Unforgiveness severs unity. We must learn to forgive our spouse quickly. *Let not the sun go down on your wrath,* the Bible states. Your unforgiving heart will hinder your prayers and, therefore, your blessings.

"Therefore if you bring your gift to the altar, and there remember that your brother has something against you, leave your gift there before the altar, and go your way. First be reconciled to your brother, and then come and offer your gift." (Matthew 5:23-24).

The unforgiven also has a responsibility because he is also yoked. He is bound by the unforgiveness of his brother. Unforgiveness is so dangerous that the person that is not forgiven is also not free.

"I don't want your gift," God says, "Your brother is upset with you, go and make it right."

It did not say you have something against your brother. It says your brother has something against you.

If your brother has something against you, it hinders your prayer. The unforgiveness of others can leave you feeling crippled and stifled; only God can cause you to break free from this feeling. This is because unforgiveness also holds the unforgiven bound. God places a responsibility on the shoulders of the unforgiven, *make it right with your brother*, He says.

We also are sometimes guilty of knowing that our offensive attitude hurt our brother and make him bitter, and yet we do nothing about it. Remember God is not accepting your gift. You have to make it right with your brother first.

Right after Jesus taught the principle of agreement in Matthew 18:19-20, Peter asked in Matthew 18:21, *"How many times must we forgive Jesus, seven?"* Jesus' answer was, *"Seventy times seven,"* in other words, as often as you are offended. Jesus knew that unforgiveness is so terribly binding and brings such hindrance to your salvation, He wanted to stress the point that it must not be allowed.

The enemy has successfully infiltrated the church, marriages, friendships, partnerships, and every relationship, with his tangled web of unforgiveness. We must recognize it and begin making every effort to get rid of this sin that holds so many bound. We are hindered in so many ways by unforgiveness.

CHAPTER 8

The Power That Sets You Free

"Then said Jesus to those Jews which believed on him, if ye continue in my word, then are ye my disciples indeed; and ye shall know the truth, and the truth shall make you free. They answered him, we be Abraham's seed, and were never in bondage to any man: how sayest thou, ye shall be made free? Jesus answered them, verily, verily, I say unto you whosoever committeth sin is the servant of sin. And the servant abideth not in the house for ever: but the Son abideth ever. If the Son therefore shall make you free, ye shall be free indeed" (John 8:31-36).

You cannot be rid of any sin unless you are aware that you are in sin and repent. Knowledge of the truth is what sets you free. Jesus said,

"You shall know the truth and the truth shall set you free."

How do we know the truth?

We know the truth through knowledge of the Word of God which says, *if ye continue in my word, then are ye my disciples indeed.*

After you come to the knowledge of the truth you must obey, *whosoever commit sin is the servant of sin.* In your total obedience to the Word of God, you will be made free.

We must be careful that what we know as truth is not a misconception. Head knowledge of the Word of God will do nothing to release bondage. It is the Spirit of God that illuminates and teaches us the truth. We have to depend heavily upon the Spirit to reveal the true condition of our hearts as we read the truth in God's Word about unforgiveness. It is this same Spirit that leads us into the truth that will convict us in order that we may turn from sin and change.

Freedom is a state of release from confinement or bandage.

Jesus says, you are a servant or you are bonded if you commit sin. When you are in bondage, you can only be set free by a source greater than that which holds you bound. Truth now becomes the force that will release you.

Let us look at the truth about the power of the blood of Jesus:

There is nothing from which the redemptive blood of Christ cannot set you free. He died so that you can be free from all sins. The blood of Jesus can make you free from hurt and pain. There are some that have been deeply wounded, even from a child. You have been abused, neglected, ignored, and abandoned. You never knew the love of a mother, or a father perhaps. There are those reading this book that is entangled in an entire life of suffering and abuse. Just when you thought you escaped the abuse of your childhood you are now trapped in abuse by your spouse. You are constantly hurt by those who are supposed to love you. There are those who would give their life for a friend, only to be hurt by that very friend to whom you gave your all. There are those who have been molested, raped, and beaten by the very persons who claim they love you. I could list a million examples here of people who have been severely hurt and mistreated. No matter how severe or mild the situation that brought you pain, the blood of Jesus Christ can set you free. You can be free from hurt; you can be free from unforgiveness.

"Therefore Jesus also, that He might sanctify the people with His own blood, suffered outside the gate." (Hebrews 13:12).

"For if the blood of bulls and goats and the ashes of a heifer, sprinkling the unclean, sanctifies for the purifying of the flesh, how much more shall the blood of Christ, who through the eternal Spirit offered Himself without spot to God, cleanse your conscience from dead works to serve the living God?" (Hebrews 9:13-14).

When you are wounded and bound by unforgiveness the power of the blood of Jesus can cleanse, heal, and make you free again. It can purge, or cleanse your very conscience and allow you liberty to serve God. Sometimes our minds plague us, and we cannot get rid of the feeling of hurt, self loathing, resentment, and all that comes with unforgiveness. Our consciences just will not set us free, the torture of the hurtful incidents plague us constantly. **You can be set free by the power of the blood.**

"And from Jesus Christ, who is the faithful witness, and the first begotten of the dead, and the prince of the kings of the earth. Unto him that loved us, <u>and washed us from our sins in his own blood</u>, and hath made us kings and priests unto God and his Father; to him be glory and dominion forever and ever. Amen" (Revelation 1:5-6).

The power of the blood of Jesus has been always potent. It will never lose its effect, or ability to save and set free. If you know that you are held bound by unforgiveness, it is time to go before God and ask for cleansing by the blood. It is time to break free.

Seeing you have now gained knowledge of the power of the blood of Jesus. **Let us practice application of this truth for our freedom:**

"Out of my distress I called on the Lord. The Lord answered me and set me free" (Psalms 118:5).

Unforgiveness becomes distressing and sometimes overwhelming to both the one who has not forgiven and the one who is not forgiven. There comes a point when you have to cry out to God for freedom from a heart bound by unforgiveness. This is no easy battle, and nothing that can be gotten over easily once the damage is done. Now that you know that the blood of Jesus Christ can set you free; it is your willingness to change that becomes important. It is a totally repentant heart that God seeks.

"The sacrifices of God are a broken spirit: a broken and a contrite heart, O God, thou wilt not despise" (Psalm 51:17).

Unforgiveness can leave you so broken it takes the power of the blood to bring change. Take your brokenness to God and He will heal and restore you. At times the wound of unforgiveness is so deep you feel crushed by its weight and believe you cannot break free.

"The LORD is nigh unto them that are of a broken heart; and saveth such as be of a contrite spirit" (Psalm 34:18).

"My flesh and my heart faileth: but God is the strength of my heart, and my portion forever" (Psalm 73:26).

God is a friend, and He desires to heal your broken heart. When your heart and your flesh fail then God can take over. He is the only one who never fails.

"And he said unto me, my grace is sufficient for thee: for my strength is made perfect in weakness…" (2 Corinthians 12:9).

You have to realize that you are weak. Depending on our own strength will see us failing most miserably at becoming free. Depending on the strength of God is necessary to attain freedom from unforgiveness. His grace is sufficient for you.

"Come unto me, all ye that labor and are heavy laden, and I will give you rest" (Matthew 11:28).

Wouldn't you like to have true rest from all the pent up feelings of hurt, bitterness, anger, and hate that unforgiveness brings? Jesus is saying to you. *Come to me. I am able to give you rest.* If you cry out to God for help, you will find that you will be able to break free. The power of unforgiveness will no longer hold you bound. What you need is a change of heart, a change of mind. What you need is rest.

"If the Son therefore shall make you free, ye shall be free indeed" (John 8:36).

When you go to the Son, when you have turned, when your mind has been changed, and you have decided to apply to the blood of Jesus to rid you of unforgiveness, then you will be set free.

"Stand fast therefore in the liberty wherewith Christ hath made us free, and be not entangled again with the yoke of bondage" (Galatians 5:1).

When you have been set free by the power of the blood, you must ensure that you do all to remain free. If you don't, you will be yoked again and placed once more in bondage.

"Being then made free from sin, ye became the servants of righteousness." Roman 6:18

You were first a servant of, or were being yoked (bound) by unforgiveness. Now that you are free you must become servants of righteousness. You must ensure at all times that you do that which is right and that which will not entangle you again.

CHAPTER 9

The Process of Overcoming

"Moreover if thy brother shall trespass against thee, go and tell him his fault between thee and him alone: if he shall hear thee, thou hast gained thy brother. But if he will not hear thee, then take with thee one or two more, that in the mouth of two or three witnesses every word may be established. And if he shall neglect to hear them, tell it unto the church: but if he neglect to hear the church, let him be unto thee as a heathen man and a publican." Matthew 18:15-17.

There is no clearer instruction in the Word of God than this. When you have found yourself in a state of unforgiveness, there is a procedure to follow in order to overcome. The first thing you must do is to go to the person who has offended you. Let them know that they have offended you. You will be surprised to know that sometimes you are hurt, and the offender is not even aware that they have offended you. The thoughtlessness of the sinful human nature causes us to say things and act in a manner that is offensive without even being aware. Therefore, it is very important that you approach your offender.

There are times when the offender knows well that they have offended you. They may be sorry, but just have no idea how to say it because of pride. The Bible now puts the onus on the one who is offended. *Go to your brother*, Jesus said, *and tell him his fault.* When someone's fault is pointed out, they may not be humble enough to accept it. This is also because of our faulty sinful nature. When you are in the process of approaching those who have offended you, pray first. Ask the Lord to speak to the heart of your offender and cause them not to be offended, or act in retaliation to what you are saying.

Even sometimes when you pray, a person who is not in total submission to the Holy Spirit will not take heed to His voice. Therefore, you may go to your offender, and they refuse to hear you. Jesus knows this and was careful to go to step two:

If he will not hear you, then take with thee one or two more that in the mouth of two or three witnesses, every word may be established.

If your offender refuses to acknowledge that he has offended you and there is still no peace between you, call one or two more brother or sister. Alot of things can transpire here. This can turn out to be a brawl or just a group of people taking sides and causing a greater rift. My suggestion is that you call mature Christian individuals, those whom you know displays godly characteristics and who are not necessarily your close friends.

The Bible instructs us to call one or two persons so that there will be atleast three persons present. *In the mouth of two or three witnesses every word will be established.* This is just a basic principle laid out in God's Word ensuring that justice is done. One witness is not enough to accuse or convict someone of a crime, according to Deuteronomy 19:15, which states,

"One witness shall not rise up against a man for any iniquity, or for any sin, in any sin that he sinneth: at the mouth of two witnesses, or at the mouth of three witnesses, shall the matter be established."

After you have followed these steps if the person still refuses to hear, the next step is to tell the church. Now your offender and you have to before the church council. The church council may or may not be able to solve the issue or bring peace. After this there is no further step you can take, the Bible says, you are allowed to consider your brother a heathen man or a sinner.

Now let me explain something to you here. In the process that was just outlined you must ensure that your heart is pure. It means then; you would have to go before the Lord asking Him for His forgiveness in not forgiving your brother, and for His help in overcoming unforgiveness. Then you begin to follow the steps. If you go through these steps with a bitter heart and not with a view to make peace, then the situation can easily escalate. Unless you know in all sincerity of heart that you are willing to forgive and make peace and that you are totally committed to obeying God's every command, don't do it. You must deal with your heart first.

Why is this important?

You can easily escalate the conflict and become deceived. You may go through the steps and all the time you are wrong, but you are doing it with one view in mind. You go through the steps bearing in mind that the Bible says you are free to consider your brother a sinner. No, that is not the reason at all for the process. The reason is to make peace. Do you notice how many steps you have to take? All of three! Do you notice how many witness you have to call, one or two, making that three or four persons, and then a council. Peace should be what you are interested in. In the process, you must do all you can in order to win your brother.

"Brethren, if a man be overtaken in a fault, you who are spiritual, restore such a one in the spirit of meekness; considering yourself, lest you also be tempted" (Galatians 6:1).

God is interested in peace and justice. He is not interested in casting away, but in restoration. All parties involved in the conflict must ensure that their interest is God's interest, that of restoration and peace. You must approach the issue with a view of getting rid of unforgiveness and not stirring up strife, which also is a sin. In the process, your brother must also be protected. The Bible exhorts us to call one or two to ensure that there is no false witness or no one trying to ensnare or lie on the other.

"If a false witness rise up against any man to testify against him that which is wrong; Then both the men, between whom the controversy is, shall stand before the LORD, before the priests and the judges, which shall be in those days; And the judges shall make diligent inquisition: and, behold, if the witness be a false witness, and hath testified falsely against his brother; Then shall ye do unto him, as he had thought to have done unto his brother: so shalt thou put the evil away from among you. And those which remain shall hear, and fear, and shall henceforth commit no more any such evil among you" (Deuteronomy 19:16-20).

"A false witness will not go unpunished, and he who speaks lies will not escape." (Proverbs 19:5).

God is not interested in a group of people taking sides against their brother with a view of accusing and throwing him out. Giving false statements and bringing false accusation against anyone is also a dangerous sin. Be careful to tread lightly in the process.

There is something else I must explain. There will be people who blatantly refuse to hear. You have tried all you can; you have gone through the process prayerfully, you are sure your heart is right before God, but your offender just will not make peace. After the council of the church has judged, in all fairness and righteousness according to God's Word, if the person refuses to hear, it is the responsibility of the council, or head of the church to consider him a heathen or a sinner.

Don't be hasty to make that decision on your own. Go on the advice of the pastor or council. If they say, *we will revisit the issue*, and if the person still remains a member of the church under the leadership of the pastor, then you have done all you know to do, and you are free. Your submission to the leadership of the church and their decision is important. Do not become rebellious against the authority of the church because of any decisions, or instructions given to you, or made by them, even if the decision, in your opinion, is wrong. That is also a sin. I must hasten to say, following all the steps has already made your free before God. The onus is no longer with you. Ensure you maintain a clean heart before God, genuinely forgive your brother, and pray for him.

How to Deal With Your Own Heart

When you have been deeply hurt, it is not very easy to forgive. I will not even pretend that it is. What I do know is that it is possible, or God would never instruct us by His Word to do so. We need to depend on the Holy Spirit to help us deal with our hearts. The first thing you must do when you have found that you have unforgiveness is to go before God. You must go when you are totally ready to obey His commands. Then you must repent of your unforgiving heart and ask God to help you to change your mind, and make your heart new. When you go to address God, your heart must be in total submission to His will. Therefore, in asking forgiveness you must be forgiving. Your prayer should go something like this:

Lord, I am willing and ready to obey your commands of forgiveness as outlined in your Word. I know I was wrong to harbor unforgiveness in my heart, help me to forgive my brother. I repent of my sin of unforgiveness. I now ask for your forgiveness.

The process as outlined in Matthew 18:15-17, and explained above, helps you make peace and win your brother. That is why Jesus said, *if he shall hear thee, thou hast gained thy brother.* In approaching this process, you should have already forgiven your brother. This total submissive and forgiving heart is what will assist you in making peace. If you need to spend some time before God asking for His help in cleansing your heart and bringing you to a point of forgiveness, please do so. Don't get off your knees, or stop praying until you feel you have truly reached a point of forgiveness. Your willingness and submission to God will break every chain that holds you bound.

How to Deal with Someone Who is out of Your Life

For someone who is now out of your life, you obviously can no longer go through the process of peace as outlined above. Therefore, you must deal with your heart as stated above. You must, in going before God, ask Him to remove all the hurt and pain and help you to forgive your offender. Sometimes, those whom we have not forgiven are not even alive anymore. People die without receiving forgiveness. You can still be free, and you can still forgive and let go of the past hurts and pain. It may be necessary for you to say out loud what the person has done to you.

Saying what the offense is may be necessary for your healing. This allows you to face that which you are hurt by. Some people cannot admit that they are hurt, and some people may know they are, but it is very painful to say it out loud. Saying it out loud is a way of breaking free from it.

I found that when I spoke about the people in my life that hurt me, it was very painful but also freeing. For some people, it may be necessary to talk to someone about your hurt or pain, especially if the offender is out of your life, and there is no way for you to talk to them about hurting you. Ensure that when you talk to anyone, it is with a view to overcome the hurt, and not to criticize or bring down the offender. Ensure that you talk to a mature friend that will give you council according to God's Word, or to a pastor, or a counselor. You may just need to let it out. If you are not comfortable talking to anyone, the greatest listener is God. Pour out your heart before Him, He understands. Remember the blood of Jesus Christ can set free and cleanse from all sin.

"In whom we have redemption through his blood, even the forgiveness of sins" (Colossians 1:14).

So even without the presence of the offender it is the blood of Jesus that cleanses. It just takes a repentant heart and a heart willing to obey God.

If you are the offender, you also have a responsibility as outlined in Matthew 5:23-26:

"Therefore if thou bring thy gift to the altar, and there rememberest that thy brother hath ought against thee; Leave there thy gift before the altar, and go thy way; first be reconciled to thy brother, and then come and offer thy gift. Agree with thine adversary quickly, whiles thou art in the way with him; lest at any time the adversary deliver thee to the judge, and the judge deliver thee to the officer, and thou be cast into prison. Verily I say unto thee, Thou shalt by no means come out thence, till thou hast paid the uttermost farthing" (Matthew 5:23-26).

It is also necessary for you to overcome unforgiveness as it also bounds you. You cannot offer your gift to God if you know that you have offended your brother. You must go to your brother and ask for his forgiveness. If you don't do this, then your brother has a right to take you even before the council as outlined in the steps above. It is even worse when the offended is not your brother, or is not a Christian. They may take you before the judge (to court). My point is your responsibility is just as great as the offended, and you must also seek to overcome the vise of unforgiveness even as the offended must.

This brings me to another point. The person who is offended or who has offended may not be a Christian or attend church. In this case, you still have to forgive in order to be free. If you are the offended you can only follow the process to step two. However, you must still deal with your heart, forgive and seek to make peace. If the person is no longer in your life the same process of going before God and forgiving as you ask forgiveness holds true. If you are the offender, it is wise for you to make peace quickly with the one you have offended.

Please note that the process of being set free and forgiving is much more difficult for someone who does not have a personal relationship with Christ. In fact, it is **ALMOST** impossible. It is advised therefore that your first ask Christ into your heart, make him Lord of your life, and then ask Him to help you with unforgiveness.

CHAPTER 10

Living a Life Free from Unforgiveness

Do you remember the process that takes you to unforgiveness as outlined in chapter two of this book? The process starts with anger, then hurt, then unforgiveness. In order to live a life of unforgiveness, you must seek to eliminate anger and hurt. Getting rid of these two things will save you the trouble and allow you to live a life free from unforgiveness.

"The discretion of a man deferreth his anger; and it is his glory to pass over a transgression" (Proverbs 19:11).

This is simply saying your discretion will make you slow to anger, and it is good to overlook wrong. This Scripture is teaching us to eliminate anger.

Discretion is simply the ability to decide responsibly. You must decide in any given situation that you will not be angry. Again, this is not easy to do, but it is possible. The Bible exhorts us to be slow to anger (James 1:19) and instructs us that anger does not yield righteousness (James 1:20). If the truth of God's Word sets us free, then we must endeavor to know the truth and be willing to obey such truth.

"He that is slow to wrath is of great understanding: but he that is hasty of spirit exalteth folly" (Proverbs 14:29).

Simply put, you act foolishly when you get angry easily, but if you are able to control anger it proves you are wise and of an understanding heart. You must get wisdom, knowledge, and understanding by asking for it of God, and then by studying God's Word and obeying it. You must deliberately practice self control because this is what is required of you by God. The Bible exhorts us that when we become Christians we must control, or bring into subjection the flesh.

"But I keep under *my body*, and bring it **into subjection**," stated Paul in 1 Corinthians 9:27.

Who should bring your body under subjection?

You!

Of course, you may need the help of the Holy Spirit, but it is you who must do it. You must actively practice not to become angry. Remember anger is not only the blurting out of words or acting out, you can have anger in your heart too.

"Because the carnal mind is enmity against God; for it is not subject to the law of God, nor indeed can be" (Romans 8:7).

"For if you live according to the flesh you will die, but if by the Spirit you put to death the deeds of the body, you will live" Romans 8:13.

What the Scripture is saying is if you set your mind on doing things that are fleshly, or of yourself, and refuse to submit to the God's commands, you become an enemy of God. Verse 13 says, if you live as the flesh you will die (a spiritual death which means separation from God). However, if you put to death or bring under subjection and control the flesh you will live. This applies to every area of the Christian life, but right now we are dealing with anger. Exercise self control.

It is possible not to be angry and still be hurt. You can totally be stung by words or action of someone and even though self control and wisdom allows you not be angry, you are still hurt. You also have to train yourself not to be offended. Let us look at Proverbs 19:11 again. The second part says,

"...it is his glory to pass over a transgression."

Your discretion or ability to decide responsibly can also allow you to pass over the transgression of the one hurling insults, or acting in a manner to cause hurt. You can decide I am not going to be hurt by his words or action. Again, this takes an enormous amount of self control, but it is possible.

The best remedy yet is love!

"But also for this very reason, giving all diligence, add to your faith virtue, to virtue knowledge, to knowledge self-control, to self-control perseverance, to perseverance godliness, to godliness brotherly kindness, and to brotherly kindness love. For if these things are yours and abound, you will be neither barren nor unfruitful in the knowledge of our Lord Jesus Christ," (2 Peter 1:5-8).

This Scripture is very important as it outlines for us some steps. Now that you are in the faith or have become a Christian you must add virtue, knowledge, self control, perseverance, godliness with brotherly kindness, and brotherly kindness with love. I listed them again to show you clearly the steps.

Virtue is your high standard of behavior. When you become a Christian your behavioral pattern ought to change. You must seek to get knowledge by studying God's Word, and this will assist you to have self control. Then you must be consistent, or persevere in displaying these godly behaviors. After that, you must start showing kindness to your brothers, and then start showing love. Ultimately, your whole life must change when you become a child of God. This is what this Scripture is saying. Ultimately too, you must have love for your brother. If you love your brother, it will be easy to pass over his transgression (refer to chapter 6). Love which covers a multitude of sin will help you to avoid hurt. Your love for your brother will keep you from being offended by him.

This holds true for anyone else. You must also love those who are not Christians. If the love of God is in your heart, you will not be so easily offended by anyone. Love will always prevail in any circumstance. Remember, it is your responsibility to win the loss for Christ. That should be at the forefront of your mind before even thinking of taking offense and becoming hurt. Ask God for His love and allow love to keep you from offense.

Of course, there are times when we have not successfully avoided anger or hurt. We are all prone to error and frailty. However, to live free of unforgiveness, you must address issues quickly. Don't allow your hurt feeling to fester into unforgiveness. The moment you find that you become angry or hurt address the matter.

Don't let the sun go down on your wrath (Ephesians 4:26), the Bible exhorts.

There is a reason for this. Hurt feeling can quickly develop into unforgiveness as your mind becomes engaged in battle. The devil will play on that hurt feeling and feed your mind with negative thoughts in order to cause you to sin. Don't allow it. Go to your offender quickly; address the matter of your own heart quickly.

"Submit yourselves therefore to God. Resist the devil, and he will flee from you" (James 4:7).

You need to submit yourself to God by doing what He commands in His Word, and resist the temptations of the devil to do otherwise.

Living a life of unforgiveness is both possible and freeing. As always my encouragement is a heart submitted to doing God's will and a total dependence of the Holy Spirit's guide.

"I can do all things through Christ which strengtheneth me" Philippians 4:13.

This is not a cliché it is the truth according to God's Word. You are able to do all things through Christ. You can live a life free from unforgiveness!

Other titles by Gillian Henriques Include:

In His Presence

A Conversation with God – Roses and Thorns

Hers to Treasure

Follow me at:

http://www.sistersinchristworldwide.org/

https://www.facebook.com/gillian.henriques

https://www.facebook.com/SistersInChristFellowshi
p

https://www.goodreads.com/GillianHenriques

Email: sicwfellowship@gmail.com

Made in the USA
Lexington, KY
17 April 2017